Listen!

FRANCES ITANI

Listen!

Grass Roots Press

Grass Roots Press gratefully acknowledges the financial support for its publishing programs provided by the following agencies: the Government of Canada through the Canada Book Fund and the Government of Alberta through the Alberta Foundation for the Arts.

Grass Roots Press would also like to thank ABC Life Literacy Canada for their support. Good Reads® is used under licence from ABC Life Literacy Canada.

Library and Archives Canada Cataloguing in Publication

Itani, Frances, 1942–
    Listen! / Frances Itani.

(Good reads)
ISBN 978-1-926583-81-5

    1. Readers for new literates. I. Title.
II. Series: Good reads series (Edmonton, Alta.)

PS8567.T35L58 2012   428.6'2   C2012–902308-6

Printed and bound in Canada.

For Lisa, Terry, Dakota, and Sam,
all part of this story-telling family

Chapter One

Listen and Worry

"Listen!" said Roma. "Listen! Keep your ears and eyes open. You have to know what's going on."

But she was talking to herself.

She looked out the train window at the night rushing by. When she spoke, her own face looked back at her from the dark window. She travelled by train because she liked to have time alone. She had booked her own tiny bedroom, a roomette, in a sleeping car. During the day, her bed folded up against the wall. In the evening, the bed pulled down. Her roomette also had a toilet and sink. An hour earlier, she had eaten dinner in the restaurant car of the train. Now, at nine-thirty, Roma was tired.

Four hours earlier, she'd waved goodbye to her husband and their daughter, Katie. Her husband had held Katie up to the train window. Katie had pressed her hand against the glass from outside. Inside the train, Roma had fitted her palm to Katie's. The train had pulled away, and Katie's face had disappeared.

Roma knew that her daughter would be fine. Sometimes, she brought her along on trips. But now, in October, Katie had to stay home to go to school.

The trip would take sixteen hours total. In the morning, Roma would arrive in Montreal. Her sister, Liz, would meet her at the Montreal station. Roma planned to stay with Liz for the next five days.

Roma had taken time off work for this trip. She worked at an outpatient clinic in a small hospital. She also interpreted for deaf patients who came into the hospital. Roma knew American Sign Language—ASL—a language she had learned as a child.

Liz had a special reason for inviting Roma to Montreal. She wanted to introduce her to two friends. The four women would meet for dinner at

Liz's home the next evening. They planned to share some of their stories.

*

Because she had little space, Roma undressed while sitting on the bed. She checked the lock on the sliding door of her roomette. She didn't want anyone walking in during the night. The train gave a jerk, and she lost her balance for a moment. She changed into a nightgown and placed her shoes on an overhead rack. Her purse hung on a hook beside the shoe rack. Every bit of space was used in this tiny roomette.

She stretched her legs and wiggled her feet under the covers, hoping to soften the crisp sheets. With two pillows behind her back, she sat up in bed and tried to relax. But she knew she couldn't sleep. She kept thinking back to her childhood. Had she ever had a childhood? Maybe not.

Roma tried to remember her life when she'd been Katie's age. Seven years old. At seven, Roma had duties that her daughter would never have. At seven, at four, even at two years of age, Roma had to be responsible. Her ears had listened for two people because her mother's ears did not hear.

Roma and Liz were hearing daughters of a deaf mother. Mam, as they called her, had suffered an illness as a baby, and that is when she'd become deaf. Roma was her first-born child. When Roma was nineteen months old, Liz was born. Not long after that, Roma began to report. Every time Liz cried, Roma had to let Mam know.

"Mam. Baby crying." The first sentence Roma ever spoke. She pulled at Mam's skirt to get her attention. She already knew that she had to face her so that Mam could read her lips.

"Mam. Baby crying."

Her mother walked to the crib and picked up the baby.

From her earliest childhood, Roma had to listen. She listened, and told Mam what was going on. That was her job. Mam needed her.

Roma's father was not deaf. A hearing man, he worked out of town Monday to Friday, and came home on weekends. He worked for the railroad, but he died in an accident when Roma was only seven. After his death, Mam relied on Roma even more.

Roma and Liz grew up in Ontario, on the edge of a town called Manor. Their house was old and small, and close to the Manor River. A dirt path along the side of the house led to the shore. As children, the two girls spent hours beside the river. Playing, laughing, arguing, sharing secrets. All the things sisters do.

But somehow, at some time, Roma began to worry. She grew up being worried. How did that happen? When Mam was alone, Roma worried. She worried when she left home, and even before she left. Would Mam remember to lock the front and back doors? What if someone tried to break into the house? Would Mam remember to add coal to the stove? Had someone ordered the coal for her?

Who worried about Mam after Roma finished school and left town? Who became the listener after Roma and Liz both moved away?

*

Roma loved to travel by train. She liked having her own private roomette. Dark shadows flew by in the night. She pulled the stiff blind down so no one could see in from outside. When the train rocked from side to side, Roma rocked with the motion. She listened to the *clack-clack* of the wheels.

As she thought of the sound, she thought of Mam again. During Roma's childhood, her family did not own a car. Mam sometimes travelled by train to visit deaf friends in Belleville. She always took Roma and Liz with her on those trips.

One summer, the train took them as far as Toronto. Roma remembered how the train had chugged forward. And how her body had rocked back and forth when she walked in the aisle. She remembered the seats, with their high backs. She had sipped cool water from small paper cups. Travel by train was a huge adventure for a child.

Roma tried to imagine how Mam might have described the train. Mam couldn't hear sounds, but she had *felt* the train. Her entire body would have sensed the turning wheels. She'd have felt every shudder and shake. Through her hands, her arms, her feet, her legs, her skin. Sometimes, the train made a loud bump. Mam did not look outside to see the reason for the bump. Instead, she looked to Roma's lips for an explanation. She expected her daughter to have the information.

Mam had always stayed silent during train trips. She feared that she would speak too loudly. Many years before, at a special school for deaf children, Mam had learned to use sign language and to use her voice. Her teachers had told her, "You can't hear yourself speak. You must learn to keep your voice low." When Mam travelled, she was afraid she would forget to control her voice.

So Roma listened for her. She told Mam the station stops the train conductor called out. When the conductor asked where they were going, Roma stepped forward to reply.

✳

The motion of the train was finally making Roma sleepy. She smoothed the wrinkled bedding and looked up. Her purse swung back and forth. Inside the purse was a small white envelope. In the envelope she had placed an old black and white photo.

Liz had asked Roma to choose one photo to bring with her to Montreal. The next evening, Liz's two friends would also bring photos to the dinner party. They would all tell stories about growing up and about deafness in their families.

Roma's photo used to belong to Mam. It had faded, and one edge was torn. When Mam died, just six months earlier, Roma and Liz had taken care of the funeral. They'd cleaned the old house to get it ready for sale. In a drawer in Mam's bedroom, they'd found the photo. Roma's childhood face peered out of one tiny corner.

Roma couldn't remember her parents taking pictures. They had owned a Kodak camera, but they had no extra money to buy or develop film. Even so, one family album had been filled. Someone must have taken photos. Roma wished she'd asked questions about the album when her mother was alive. Now, both her parents had died, and there was no one left to ask.

"Listen!" Roma told herself again. This time, she could hear Mam's voice in her memory. Exactly the way Mam used to speak. Hundreds, thousands of times, Roma had heard the same word: *Listen!*

Chapter Two

___

Reporting

As a child, Roma often spoke for her deaf mother. Most strangers could not understand Mam's voice. But Roma could understand every word Mam spoke. Hers was the first voice Roma ever heard.

Roma also became Mam's ears. As soon as she could talk, she told her mother what was going on.

She told Mam when footsteps walked up to the front of the house.

When someone knocked at the door.

When Mam's dog raised his head and began to bark.

What the minister said in church.

When the phone rang, Roma picked up the receiver. She listened to the caller's voice and passed on the message. She told the caller Mam's reply.

Roma was always in the middle. Listen and tell. Tell and listen. She became her mother's ears and voice.

When the kitchen sink leaked, Roma phoned the plumber.

"I am four years old and my mother is deaf," Roma said into the phone. "Our sink is broken and we need a plumber."

She gave the plumber the house address. At an early age, she had to memorize her address and phone number.

Roma also went shopping with Mam. "A pound of sliced baloney," she told the grocer. "Sliced thin, please. A small jar of mustard and a can of beans." The grocer did not understand Mam's voice.

At Woolworth's lunch counter, Roma ordered a cup of tea for Mam.

In the shoe store, she told the clerk the size of Mam's feet. "Size eight, please. My mother wears size eight."

Sometimes, a sales clerk said, "What's the matter with your mother, little girl?"

Roma replied, "There's nothing wrong with my mother." And there wasn't. To Roma, Mam's deafness was normal.

When hearing people visited the house, Roma had another job. Her mother told her to remember what everyone talked and laughed about. She did not want to miss anything.

"Listen!" she told Roma. "Listen to what the others are saying."

Mam and Roma both knew that visitors often spoke quickly. Or changed the subject suddenly. Or turned away, and their lips could not be read. A man might have a beard or a mustache that covered his lips. A woman might put a hand up to her face when she spoke.

Later, after cousins and aunts and uncles went home, Mam sat Roma down. "What did he say? What did she say? Tell me the news," she said.

And Roma tried to remember and report.

Mam wanted to know everything.

If visitors knew how to use sign language, Roma did not have to be in the middle. Mam had learned to lip-read and to use American Sign Language as a small child. The special school she had attended was the Ontario School for the Deaf in Belleville. Back then, deaf children lived at the school ten months of the year. They were allowed to go home during summer, and sometimes at Christmas. They studied the same subjects as all Ontario students, but they had special classes, too. Some deaf students learned to use their voices and to lip-read. All had to learn sign language. For ten years, Mam lived in the girls' residence and made many good friends.

When Roma and her sister, Liz, were born, Mam taught them to sign. The two sisters used their hands to create language from the time they were babies.

But most hearing visitors who came to their house did not know American Sign Language.

While Roma was growing up, she was the bridge between hearing and deaf worlds.

"Listen!" Mam said. "Tell me what is happening."

Roma reported back. If she wanted to help Mam, she had to know what was going on.

Chapter Three

On the Train

Roma heard a loud blast from the train's horn and stretched her legs again. The train was slowing, maybe stopping at a small station. She lifted the blind to look and saw nothing but darkness. She pushed the blind back down and sank into the pillows again. The trip had begun to raise memories of events she hadn't thought of for years. Maybe she should phone her sister. She and Liz talked on the phone every week. They always had. Ever since they'd left home and married and had children of their own.

As the train began to move faster again, Roma punched in the numbers on her cell phone. Liz sounded sleepy when she answered. A buzzing noise could be heard through the phone.

"Roma?" said Liz. "Is that you? It's late. Where are you calling from?"

"I don't know," Roma said. "I'm on the train, but I don't know exactly where. There's nothing to see outside but the night. The train is speeding along the track, and I'm sitting in my bed."

"I'll be at the station to pick you up," said Liz. "But not until morning."

"I know. I'm just thinking about things."

"What things?"

"I've been thinking of Mam and how much I miss her. I've been thinking about you, too. And of all the times I worried about Mam."

"I know you worried. Even after we left home, you used to phone me," Liz said. "You'd say: 'What if Mam lets the stove go out? What if the pipes in her house freeze in winter? What if? What if?'"

"Well, I couldn't change overnight," said Roma. "I also worried that someone would break into our old house."

"Mam always had a dog," Liz said. "You know that. When one dog died, she got another. When you and I weren't home, the dogs acted as Mam's ears. She loved every one of those dogs."

"Her first dog was Chip," Roma said. "A mutt Father brought home one summer. You weren't very old at the time."

"I remember Chip. He became Mam's special dog," said Liz.

"He didn't look dangerous or mean," said Roma. "He wasn't even very big. He only reached as high as Mam's knees."

"He looked like a dog pirate," Liz said. "He had a black patch around one eye."

"Chip didn't like you and me," said Roma.

"But he loved Mam," said Liz. "She was the only one allowed to pat him."

"Chip threatened to bite everyone else," Roma added. "Even us."

"Father trained him to scare strangers."

"You and I weren't strangers," said Roma. "But Chip was Mam's warning signal. If anyone came up the walk, he raised his head and barked."

"Then he ran to Mam and brushed against her leg," said Liz.

"Why did he try to bite us?" Roma said. "We lived there."

"Mam kept telling us not to be afraid," said Liz. "We *were* afraid."

Liz started to laugh. "Chip chased us up onto the kitchen table. Do you remember?"

Roma started laughing, too. "That happened a few years after Father died."

"Mam went for a walk with Aunt Helen after supper," said Liz.

"And Chip stayed behind to guard us. Mam never believed that Chip hated us, but he chased you and me up onto the table. Once he forced us up there, he wouldn't let us down."

"You reached over and grabbed the broom that leaned against the wall," said Liz.

"I shook the broom and tried to scare him," said Roma. "But no one could scare Chip. He stayed there, barking, baring his teeth. We finally had to sit on the table and wait."

"Mam was back in five or ten minutes."

"She blamed us," said Roma. "She said that if we'd stop being afraid, Chip would leave us alone."

But Roma and Liz had hated Chip, and the dog had hated them.

"The next dog was better," said Liz. "He was a collie, wasn't he?"

"A smart collie," said Roma. "He always knew when Mam was alone in the house."

"He knew she couldn't hear him bark," said Liz. "So when he was outside, he learned how to get back in. He jumped up near the kitchen window and scratched at the glass and moved his paws. Mam saw the movement, and opened the back door."

"If he didn't show his paws, he didn't get in," said Roma.

"All of Mam's dogs had to be smart," said Liz.

"I sometimes wonder how any of us survived," Roma said. "Including the dogs. How did Mam manage all those years? Especially after Father died."

"She managed. And you and I couldn't stay home forever. We went to school and studied hard and got jobs and moved away. Now we have families of our own," said Liz.

"I hope my Katie never worries about me," said Roma. "Not the way I worried about Mam. I want Katie to have a childhood. I don't want her to have any guilt about me."

"She won't," said Liz. "Now, go to sleep, Roma. Get some rest on the train. We survived childhood.

You did your best, and so did I. Would we have changed our lives if we'd had the chance? Probably not. I'll see you in the morning, at the station."

Roma said goodnight to Liz and turned out the light in her roomette.

Chapter Four

The Language They Used

The wheels of the train hurried along the tracks. *Click-a-clicka, click-a-clicka.* Then there was a bump, followed by another. *Click-a-clicka* started all over again. The same rhythm as before.

The rhythm reminded Roma of songs she sang to Katie. She loved to sing to her daughter. Lullabies and rhymes and songs of all kinds.

> *There was an old woman*
> *Who lived in a shoe*

and

Hush little baby, don't say a word,
Papa's going to buy you a mockingbird

and

When you wake, you shall have
All the pretty little horses.

As a child, Roma had heard none of these.

Mam did not sing because she had never heard a song. Roma's father worked away from home most of the time. That's why Roma learned lullabies and nursery rhymes only after Katie's birth. She sang them as if they were prizes she and Katie had won.

Mam, because of her deafness, had no way of knowing songs or rhymes. These had not been part of a deaf child's life. The earliest language Mam had spoken was with her hands. She read lips, too, and received language through her eyes. Alert and quick, she didn't miss much, but she could not sing or rhyme. She did know stories, however. Stories she told with her hands.

Liz and Roma watched the hand-stories and signed back to their mother. Moving hands and fingers filled the air with language. From high chair, crib, and stroller, the girls used their baby hands to speak. They learned two languages: the spoken word and American Sign Language. As they grew older, they spelled out names of people and places in sign language. They used the hand alphabet and became good spellers.

The house filled with visible language.

Eyebrows lifted, eyebrows lowered. Faces frowned or grinned or laughed or became serious or sad. Lips moved. Lips were read. With fingers, Roma and Liz wrote words in the air. To get Mam's attention, Roma and Liz flicked light switches off and on. They tapped Mam's arm or pulled at her skirt. They stamped their feet on hardwood floors to make the wood vibrate. Their mother felt the vibration and looked their way.

The sisters pounded their little fists on tables and chairs. They banged at walls. Doors slammed. Everyone was noisy. That's what their house was like. Noisy.

Their mother swept the floor, picked up a waste basket, and crashed it down. Mam did not know she was making so much noise. Upstairs, Roma and Liz shouted to each other from room to room. Mam did not know they shouted behind her back. The sisters could be wicked, and Mam wouldn't know. How could she know, when she was deaf?

When the girls were in the same room as Mam, their behaviour changed. They did not shout. Their mother was too quick for them. If they talked behind her back, she somehow knew.

"Roma! What did you say?" Mam would ask. "I know you said something."

"Nothing," Roma lied.

"Liz? What did you say?"

"Nothing," Liz lied.

But Mam knew they had spoken. She could tell by looking at their faces.

*

Roma thought about the kitchen in their house. The noisiest place of all. When Roma was a child, Mam banged pots and pans and lids and spoons. Mam taught the girls to bake. On baking days, dishes piled high in the sink. The heat of the oven filled the room. Windows clouded over with steam.

The stove in the kitchen burned coal in winter, wood in summer. On hot days when they had to cook, they burned a few sticks of wood. Just enough to heat food or cook a fast meal. In winter, the stove had to be kept going all the time.

Mam had a book called the Cook's Book. She had written all the recipes by hand. She had been collecting these recipes ever since she'd lived at the School for the Deaf.

Liz and Roma wore long aprons when they baked. Roma picked up the Cook's Book and read aloud. "Two yolks eggs beaten up."

They laughed and laughed. Mam read their lips and laughed, too. "Let's beat up the eggs," Mam said.

"Stir cookies and drop," Roma read.

They laughed some more. Liz pretended to drop cookie dough on the floor.

Mam had written in the Cook's Book: *Roll in white eggs.*

Did it matter if they cooked with white eggs or egg whites? Mam didn't seem to care. That was all part of her private written language.

One day Roma learned to bake a cake. "How many walnuts should I put in?" she asked.

"Ten cents' worth," Mam replied. Roma knew exactly what her mother meant.

They baked on weekends to prepare dessert for the girls' school lunches. Roma did more baking after Mam went out to work. A year after Roma's father died, Mam began to look for a job. She found work at a shirt factory and sewed at a machine all day. At the factory, she did not have to use her voice. She could do the job, even though she was deaf. One other deaf woman worked there, and she and Mam became good friends. The two women ate lunch together and used ASL as their language. By four o'clock every afternoon, Mam arrived home from work.

At nine years of age, Roma could make lunches for school. She baked cookies and cakes. She heated leftovers and set the table for supper. She knew how to scramble eggs, boil eggs, and fry eggs. Roma was best at making eggs on toast.

*

The family had a visible language for sickness during Roma's childhood. The sickness language started with Mam's worried face. Then Mam felt Roma's forehead to check for fever and sent her up to bed.

Mam banged around the kitchen. When Roma heard footsteps on the stairs, she knew what was coming. Mam carried up a bowl of warm milk sprinkled with pepper. Roma had to drink the milk and pepper because her mother believed this could cure almost anything.

After Roma drank the last drop, Mam brought out the scrapbook. Looking through the scrapbook was part of being sick. The crisp covers. The *slap-slap* of paper. Pages stuffed with Christmas cards, old valentines, and birthday cards. Pictures cut from magazines, pasted to the pages. Pictures of animals and food and flowers. Pictures of kings and queens. Pictures of fancy clothes Roma's family would never have money to buy. Colourful pictures of places they would never see. Looking at the scrapbook was like taking a trip to a different world.

Mam sat at the edge of the bed, watching over Roma's shoulder as they turned the pages. Mam remembered pasting every picture. She had begun to fill the pages when she'd lived at the School for the Deaf. Sometimes, a story went with a picture. Mam told these stories with her hands. She had filled the scrapbook with stories from her life as a deaf child. The scrapbook, brought out only when Roma and Liz were sick, became part of the family language.

Chapter Five

The Thimble Man

Liz met Roma at the station when the train pulled in. The two sisters spent the afternoon catching up and preparing food. Liz's husband and children went out for the evening, and now the women had the place to themselves.

When Liz's friends arrived, she introduced them as Jessie and Eve. She explained that her friends belonged to a group called CODA: Children of Deaf Adults. A few months earlier, Liz had contacted CODA in Montreal. She missed Mam, and she wanted to talk to other children of deaf parents. At her first meeting, she had met Jessie and Eve. Roma had known about CODA, but had never joined.

Now, Roma looked around the cozy dining room. Her sister sat at the head of the table. Jessie worked as a sign language interpreter. Eve was an actor who sometimes worked with deaf children in a theatre group.

After the four women had eaten and talked for a while, Liz served dessert. Each of the women had a photo propped next to her plate. They planned to share their stories while having dessert and coffee.

"Who would like to go first?" Liz asked the others. She looked around the table.

Roma held up her photo. "I'll go first," she said. "My story is about something that took place long ago, but I remember it well."

"Am I in the story?" Liz wanted to know.

"You'll have to wait and see," Roma told her sister. "I'll tell the story exactly the way I remember it."

Roma passed her photo around the table.

"As you can see, there are two adult figures in my photo. Two adults outside, and a child's small round face inside, looking through a window. Hollyhocks reach up from a narrow garden below the window. The tips of their flowers can be seen from inside the kitchen. I remember the colours, all pinks and whites.

"I am the child at the window. My mother is one of the adults, and she is standing by the side of our old house. The Manor River is just out of sight.

"I should explain that Liz and I always called our mother *Mam*. I'm not sure how that happened. We called her Mam from the time we were babies. Maybe that's the way our deaf mother said the word *Mom*. But however this happened, everyone knew her as Mam. Even our father called her Mam.

"In the photo, Mam is wearing white shorts and white sandals. Her back is to the camera, and her head is tilted. She has just washed her long, black hair. She is holding a hairbrush and trying to dry her hair in the sun. From outside, she is using the window as a mirror. You can see in the reflection that she has a huge smile on her face. I like to think she's smiling at me. Because I am in the kitchen, sitting on a stool and looking out.

"I don't know who is behind the camera. Maybe a friend of Mam's. Maybe a neighbour who lives in a house along the river. Anyway, someone took the picture on a weekday, when my father was away at work. I know this because, in the picture, I am doing my job."

*

Roma's story:

My job was to wait for my baby sister to wake. When I heard Liz wake up, I had to let Mam know. I would do this by making the sign for "baby" through the window. Mam would see me signing, and she would come and lift Liz out of her crib. After that, I would be allowed to go out to play.

I was four years old when the photo was taken. I know this because Mam wrote my name and the date on the back. If I was four, then Liz was two. Liz still had naps during the daytime, but I did not. Liz had her baby naps in the downstairs bedroom, where Mam had put a crib. This was a small room next to the kitchen. Every day at nap time, Mam gave Liz a baby bottle filled with milk. Liz drank the milk and went to sleep.

When Liz woke from her nap, she stood in her crib. She picked up her empty baby bottle and threw it at the door frame. In her two-year-old way, she somehow knew that Mam was deaf. She threw the bottle to get Mam's attention. She aimed it to hit the frame and land outside the bedroom door. That way, Mam would see it bounce. Liz was very smart.

Mam was smart, too. In those days, baby bottles were made of glass. So the first time Liz threw one, it broke. Mam placed a thick mat on the kitchen floor. After that, when Liz threw a bottle, it bounced off the door frame and landed on the mat. There were no more broken baby bottles after that.

But the day of this photo, Mam was outside, drying her hair. Inside, I had to sit on a stool by the window and listen for Liz. I'd become tired of waiting for her to throw her baby bottle.

Through the screen door, I heard someone's footsteps coming up the front walk. *Step, drag. Step, drag.* Only one person I knew dragged his foot to make that sound. The thimble man!

Part of the thimble man can be seen here. He is the second adult in the photo. He looks as if he's walking into the side of the picture.

The thimble man had a puffy face and wide shoulders. He had been a soldier during the last war and had been wounded in the leg. He earned his living by selling small items door to door. He sold needles, thread, shiny thimbles, and buttons. He sold ribbons and scarves and combs and hairnets and cards of safety pins. Twice a year, he came to our house.

The thimble man wore a long, heavy coat in all seasons, even in summer. He opened one side of his coat to display the items he had to sell. He had attached rows of silver thimbles of different sizes to the coat's lining. Neat rows of buttons lined up beside the thimbles. Rows of needles in small envelopes were tucked into folds of cloth. Coloured scarves hung down. Everything was attached to the lining of the thimble man's coat.

Mam sewed all our clothes. Every time the thimble man visited, she bought sewing supplies from him. Sometimes, the thimble man had treats to sell, too. For small girls, he had tiny pins shaped like wishbones. They had sparkles and coloured stones stuck to them. The thimble man had once told me that I could wish on one of his pins. If I owned one, whatever I wished for would come true. Of course, that made me want a wishbone pin. I asked for one for my next birthday. Mam told me she would buy one, but I couldn't wear it until the day I turned five.

When I saw the thimble man, I forgot about baby Liz waking up. I slid off the stool and ran out the back door. In the backyard, Mam and the thimble man were making signs to each other. The thimble man did not know sign language, so he made up his own signs. He and Mam laughed at the language they created with their hands.

We all forgot about Liz in her crib inside the house. The thimble man began to turn in circles. He held out the sides of his coat and began a slow dance. One foot dragged behind the other. With his coat open, he was as wide as two men. The sun sparkled on the wishbone pins, and scarves fluttered inside his coat. I was sure the thimble man was magic. I wanted to dance, too, and I turned circles behind him. We were both dancing outside the back door.

When I heard Liz, her cry came from far away. Mam dropped coins into the thimble man's hand. The thimble man closed his magic coat and waved goodbye. Dragging his foot behind him, he started back up the front walk. *Step, drag. Step, drag.*

Liz was screaming now, and I had never heard her scream that way before. I pulled at Mam's arm and made her look at my lips.

"Mam!" I yelled. "The baby is screaming."

Mam could see from my face that something was wrong. She saw the word *baby* on my lips. She ran into the house, but I ran in a different direction. I ran toward the sound of Liz's screams. That meant down the path that led to the river. In a moment, Mam was behind me, and then she was in front. We both saw Liz at the same time. Liz was splashing and crying. She had fallen into the river and couldn't get out.

Liz must have thrown her baby bottle when she woke up. When no one lifted her out of the crib, she climbed over the side. She walked out the front door and around the side of the house. No one saw her go down the path to the river.

Mam ran into the river, her white sandals splashing through water. She grabbed Liz and lifted her up and out of the river. Because of the danger, Mam forgot that her hands were full. She'd been holding a thimble, buttons, and the wishbone pin for my birthday. All of these had been bought from the thimble man. Now, they were at the bottom of the river.

Mam hugged Liz close to her chest and ran back to the house. Liz coughed and choked and spit up water. I ran behind. Liz was safe, and she did not drown. The three of us were all crying — Liz and Mam and I.

I knew it was my fault that Liz got out the door and went to the river. Mam did not blame me, but I believed it was my fault. I hadn't stayed on the stool to wait for Liz to wake up. Instead, I'd gone out to greet the thimble man. I had not done my job and listened. Because of this, Liz might have drowned. Because of this, my wishbone pin lay somewhere at the bottom of the river.

∗

Liz, Jessie, and Eve watched while Roma placed the photo back on the table.

"Wow. I'm glad I survived," said Liz.

"You know," said Roma, "I used to wade along the shallow edge of the river. I wanted to find the wishbone pin. I looked for it even years later, when we were in our teens. But I never found it."

"Of course you didn't," said Liz. "Just a little way from shore, the current was strong in that river. The wishbone pin was probably dragged into deeper water the moment it was dropped. It's probably at the bottom of Lake Ontario now."

"Good thing you knew enough to scream," Roma said. "Or you'd be at the bottom of Lake Ontario, too."

"Thanks a lot," said Liz. "I was only two years old. I don't even remember falling in."

"I'll never forget," said Roma. "Even though I was only four."

"I have heard part of that story before," Liz told her CODA friends. "Mam never forgave herself for forgetting about me in the crib."

"Mam and I were both guilty," said Roma.

"Well, you can stop being guilty right now," said Liz. "The world is full of people who can't forgive themselves. What good does guilt do? Nothing bad happened, did it?"

"No. You didn't drown. But I always believed it was my fault that you fell in."

"You were four years old," said Liz. "What are you talking about? You were a little child, yourself."

"Mam relied on me," Roma said. "She counted on me to tell her when you threw your baby bottle. And the wishbone pin was lost. I never did get one for my fifth birthday."

"Oh, the wishbone pin," said Liz.

"I know it's silly. All through childhood, I wondered if I'd find it. I really believed I could make a wish if I had the pin."

"What would you have wished for?" Liz asked.

Roma thought for a moment. "A wish has to be kept secret," she said. "Anyway, the pin wasn't the most important part of the story. The important part was about worrying. I always worried about Mam."

"I did, too," said Liz.

The other two women knew what Roma and Liz were talking about. Jessie and Eve had worried about their deaf parents, too.

"We became responsible children," Jessie said. "We had no choice. We had to mature early."

Chapter Six

―――――

The Berries

Jessie worked as a sign language interpreter at a community centre. She looked around the table at Roma, Liz, and Eve. "My mom and dad were born deaf," she said. "They met at a School for the Deaf in western Canada. Like your mom, they lived in residence. Three years after they finished school, they married and moved east to Ontario."

Jessie continued: "We lived near Smiths Falls when I was born. I was the first child. I had three brothers and one sister. None of us was born deaf. Even so, American Sign Language was the language we used. But we grew up with two languages in the house, ASL and spoken English. We children used our voices to speak to one another. To our parents, we signed. Most often, we used both at the same time: speech and sign. Even now, my thoughts are in pictures," Jessie said. "Everything is visual for me. When I speak, I see words in sign language. That probably happens to many hearing children of deaf parents.

"My dad had a job working in a hospital laundry. Sometimes, we wondered what our lives would be like if we were rich. We used to say: 'I wonder how rich people live?' Wondering how rich people live became a joke in our family."

Jessie held up her photo and then passed it around the table. "You'll see that I am leaning against a truck here," she said. "What you can't see clearly is the field of berries behind the truck. Rows and rows of raspberries. My story is about Mrs. Berry. A woman who was very rich."

*

Jessie's story:

The truck in the photo belonged to Mr. and Mrs. Berry. They also owned two cars, and a farm outside Smiths Falls. Everyone called them *the Berries*, even though that wasn't their real name.

The Berries raised dogs and horses as well as raspberries. Sometimes I walked past their property and thought, "So that's how rich people live." I had never been inside their big house.

The first paying job I ever had was picking berries. Mr. Berry had gone away on a business trip. Mrs. Berry needed pickers because the berries were ripe. She came to our door one evening and asked if I wanted a job. Raspberry picking would start the next day. She said she paid eight cents for every box picked. She also supplied lunch for the pickers. The job would last about three weeks.

My parents said it would be all right for me to work. They said it would be good for me to earn some money.

After Mrs. Berry left, my dad joked with me. He said, "Well, Jessie, maybe you'll find out how rich people live. Pay attention. Keep your ears open and listen! You can report back to the rest of us."

The next morning, a truck arrived to pick me up. The driver worked for the Berry family and helped out with their horses. When I climbed into the back of the truck, I saw two other students. They were friends of mine from high school and had been picked up before me. When we arrived at the berry farm, Mrs. Berry came out to greet us.

My friends and I were given stacks of empty boxes. The truck driver took us to the field and showed us where to start. We had to fill the boxes with berries and carry them to the end of the row. Full boxes were placed in large wooden flats. The flats were loaded into the back of the truck.

After five minutes of bending over bushes, I ached everywhere. My fingernails were stained dark purple. I wondered if I could last a full day. The sun became hotter and hotter. At ten o'clock, a maid carried lemonade and glasses out to the field on a tray.

The cold drink revived us. When we'd had enough, we started picking again. The maid told us that lunch would be served at twelve o'clock.

I looked up at the sun, hoping for time to pass. I didn't own a watch. When the sun was directly overhead, the maid came to the field and called us. She said we would be eating in the house.

In we went, the three of us, who could now be called berry pickers. We had red scratches on our arms and legs, and our knees were dirty. The maid showed us where to wash our hands and pointed out the dining room.

Mrs. Berry was already seated at one end of a long table. She wore a sundress with narrow straps, gold earrings, and gold bracelets. The bracelets rattled every time she moved her arms.

I counted five empty chairs at Mrs. Berry's table. Three on one side, two on the other. The maid told my two friends and me to sit along one side. Six china plates had been set out. One for Mrs. Berry, three for the pickers, and two others. I looked around to see who else would join us for lunch. I thought maybe the truck driver and the maid would sit with us.

Mrs. Berry suddenly called to her dogs, two large Irish setters. They had been waiting in the doorway, and now they raced in, wagging feathery tails. They leaped up onto the two empty chairs across the table from me. They settled into the seats as if they sat there every day. The maid came in and tied a large cloth napkin around each dog's neck. The napkins hung like triangles over the dogs' long throats.

The maid then carried in a plate of ham sandwiches made from white bread spread with mustard. The crusts had been neatly trimmed off. The sandwiches with mustard were for the humans.

The dogs stared down at their empty plates. The maid left the room and returned again. This time, she carried a plate of ham sandwiches with no mustard. These were for the dogs. She also served the dogs extra slices of ham.

I began to wonder if the maid had served enough food. I was sure the dogs would eat our sandwiches after they finished their own. But they behaved well. They gulped their food quickly but neatly. They also watched Mrs. Berry, who talked to them all through the meal. She called the dogs "darlings." She didn't have much to say to the rest of us. She didn't say one word to me. I had been picking her berries all morning, and I was hungry. I had nothing to say to her, either.

By the end of that first day of berry picking, I was exhausted. At three o'clock in the afternoon, my friends and I stopped work. The truck driver drove us home, and he picked us up again the next morning. The second day, my friends and I wore jeans to protect our legs from scratches.

The job lasted three weeks. Every day, I ate lunch with the dogs in the large dining room. I liked the dogs more than I liked Mrs. Berry.

I worked hard and earned enough money to buy clothes for school. I never wanted to see another raspberry.

But I was able to report to my family. I finally knew how rich people lived.

My deaf parents listened with great interest. We all laughed and laughed. I told them about the dogs sitting on chairs and eating off china plates.

My mom loved hearing about napkins being tied around the dogs' necks. "Imagine," she said. "Just imagine how rich people live."

"Maybe that's how hearing people live," said my dad.

I wasn't sure if he was joking or not.

*

At the end of her story, Jessie looked around Liz's table. "I knew that my family was different," she said. "We were different because both my parents were deaf. Somehow, having an inside look at a rich woman's life made me feel better. I was learning that everyone's life was different in some way."

Chapter Seven

Feet

Eve earned her living as an actor with a Montreal theatre company. Every summer, she worked with deaf children in theatre classes.

Eve passed her photo around. "You can see two girls standing by a riverbank," she said. "I am the girl on the left, and I was thirteen years old at the time. I look pretty unhappy here. After you hear my story, I think you'll understand why.

"The girl on the right is my sister, and she was eleven. We grew up just outside Belleville, close to the Moira River." She looked around the table.

"Were we all poor when we were children?" she asked the others.

Liz nodded. "Poor in some ways, maybe. Rich in others."

"Well," said Eve, "my story is about feet. Charity and feet. I was in grade seven and I was very sensitive. Both of my parents were deaf, but they were divorced. My sister and I lived with our mother. We didn't see much of our father because he had moved away. After the divorce, my mother went to work at a canning factory. She worked really hard to support us."

Eve took a deep breath, as if she had a theatre part to act. "Look at the photo and see what I'm wearing on my feet," she said.

＊

Eve's story:

During the last week of August, someone left a cardboard box on our doorstep in the night. Our mother found the box before she left for work in the morning. There was no label on the box, and we never found out who had left it.

"I hope people don't think we need charity," Mother said.

No one had ever left a box on our step before. Mother dragged it into the kitchen and opened the top. The three of us could see clothes inside.

"I have to leave or I'll be late for work," Mother told us. "You girls look through the box. There might be some good school clothes in there."

My sister and I did not own many store-bought clothes. Mostly, we wore clothes our mother sewed for us on her Singer sewing machine. She bought material and made dresses, slacks, skirts, and even coats. These were beautiful, but my sister and I badly wanted store-bought clothes.

After our mother left for work, my sister and I lifted the clothing out of the box. We pulled out sweaters, blouses, a winter coat, and four skirts. The clothes had hardly been worn. At the bottom of the box, we found a pair of boots and one pair of shoes. The boots had fur trim around the top and fit my sister perfectly. She couldn't wait to wear them.

We tried on skirts and sweaters to see what would fit. We liked everything but the shoes. These looked like old-lady shoes. We knew our mother would never wear them to work at the canning factory. Our mother was not an old lady.

I held the shoes in the air, and my sister and I both laughed. "These are such a joke," I said. The shoes were brown and heavy, with dark brown laces, and holes punched into the sides. They had thick, clunky heels, not like today's heels. They were shoes a ninety-year-old woman would wear.

When Mother came home from work that evening, she looked at every item.

"Try on the shoes," she said.

"Not me," said my sister.

"I don't mean you," said Mother. "I mean Eve."

"Not me," I told my mother. "I'll never put those ugly things on my feet."

"They're not so bad," said Mother. "You're the one who needs new shoes for school. I'm only asking you to try them on."

To my horror, the shoes fit.

"I'll never wear them," I said. "These are old-lady shoes. I am thirteen years old. No one in my class owns shoes like these."

"Your others have worn out," Mother said. "These are made of leather. Look at them. They'll be good school shoes."

School was to start the following week.

I looked to my sister for support, but she looked away.

"The shoes don't fit," I told my mother. "They hurt my feet."

"Stand up straight," my mother said. She pushed on the leather toe with her thumb. "You have extra room at the toe. A perfect fit."

"You'll never make me wear them," I said. But I said this to my mother's back.

My mother turned around and looked at my face. "Don't talk behind my back, Eve. You'll have to wear the shoes. I don't have extra money to buy new ones."

I was so angry, I ran upstairs to my bedroom. I turned on my radio and set the volume as high as it would go. Mother couldn't hear, but the loud noise made me feel better.

The next day, after Mother left for work, my sister and I walked beside the river.

"I should have thrown the shoes into the river," I said. "Mother didn't know we'd find shoes in the box. Not until she came home from work yesterday."

But I knew our mother really couldn't afford new shoes. I knew I'd have to wear the ugly shoes on the first day of school. And every day after that.

I hated getting on and off the school bus because I didn't want anyone looking at my feet. When I walked in the terrible shoes, I could hear the noise of thick heels. *Clomp, clomp, clomp.* I felt as if I had flashing lights on my feet.

I knew the other girls at school talked about my shoes. No one said anything directly to me. I was already different because my parents were divorced. I was different because my parents were deaf. I wanted to fit in, and I didn't want anyone to feel sorry for me.

After a few weeks, the heel on one of my shoes began to loosen. It wobbled on the nails that held it. I was glad the heel had started to come off. If I could make it break, I'd get new shoes after all.

I scraped the wobbly heel against rocks. I scraped it against the floor. Everywhere I went, I tried to make the heel snap off the shoe.

At school, when the weather was good, students had to line up outside. Girls in one long line, boys in another. When the bell rang, we marched inside and went to our classrooms. Our teachers followed us into the school.

In early October, rain had fallen for days, making the ground wet and muddy. Students could not line up outside the school until the rain stopped.

When the sun shone again, I took my place in line and waited for the bell to ring. I scraped my shoe along the muddy ground. I was still trying to break the heel.

To my surprise, the wobbly heel suddenly fell off. At the same moment, the school bell rang, and students ahead of me began to move. I had to start walking, so I left my heel behind, in the mud.

Now, instead of a heel, three nails stuck out of the bottom of my shoe. I had no heel, but I had nails to walk on. Every time I took a step, the nails rang out against the floor. My broken shoe made more noise than it had before the heel fell off. I tried to walk on tiptoes down the long hall. When I reached my classroom, I quickly sat at my desk.

My teacher, Mr. Peters, came up beside me and placed the heel on my desk.

"Is this yours, Eve?" he asked. "I found it in the mud outside."

I nodded, my face red with shame. Everyone stared at the big clunky heel on my desk.

I spent the rest of the afternoon trying to press the heel back onto the nails.

When I got home from school, Mother was still at the canning factory.

I took off both shoes and ran toward the river. My sister ran along beside me.

"What are you going to do?" she said. She could see the shoes in my hand.

"I'm going to throw them in the river," I told her.

"You'd better not, Eve," she said. "Mother will be upset."

"I don't care," I said. And I really didn't care.

When we reached the shore, I threw the shoes as hard as I could. I watched them bob up and down in the water before they sailed away.

The next morning, I told Mother I couldn't find my shoes. I told her I couldn't go to school.

Mother made me look in every room of the house. She made my sister look, too. We searched until the school bus arrived. Mother had to leave for work and I still had no shoes to wear.

My sister was loyal. She did not tell on me.

I stayed home from school that day, and my sister rode the school bus without me. When Mother returned home from work, we searched for the shoes again.

Mother was not happy with me, but she finally took me to the shoe store. She had to buy me a new pair of shoes.

I never told my mother about throwing the shoes into the river.

I was not proud that I did not tell the truth. But I got to own a pair of normal-looking shoes. I didn't want anyone feeling sorry for me or laughing because we were poor.

*

Because Eve knew how to perform, she made the others at the table laugh. Roma and Liz and Jessie understood Eve's story very well.

Chapter Eight

Piano

Roma's sister Liz worked as a musician and music teacher. She held up a black and white photo that Roma had seen before.

"I was sixteen in this photo," said Liz, as she passed it around the table. "Roma was eighteen and had already left home. She won a scholarship and lived in residence at university. After Roma left, I lived alone with Mam. I still had two more years of high school."

Liz continued. "The photo shows the living room of the house where Roma and I grew up. I am sitting on a piano bench, facing a piano. My hands stretch over the keyboard, and a music book is propped in front of me. But I am not looking at the notes on the page. As you can see, I'm staring down at the keys. I have a serious look on my face."

*

Liz's story:

You won't be surprised when I tell you that Mam always wished for a piano. Many of Mam's deaf friends owned pianos. Why did deaf people want pianos?

Anyway, Mam could not afford a piano. So one of our grandmothers decided to search for one. She found and bought a second-hand piano, which she gave to Mam for her fiftieth birthday.

A big moving truck arrived at our house to deliver the piano. The following week, my grandmother paid to have the piano tuned.

Mam loved that piano. Right away, she wanted me to learn to play. I banged at the keys, but Mam didn't want that. She wanted me to learn properly. Roma had left home, so I was the one who had to learn. That's what Mam thought.

I had no interest in learning piano. I wanted to listen to the radio. At my high school, I had learned the words to popular songs. I began to go to school dances with my friends. I wanted to know all the songs we danced to.

My teachers knew I could sing, and I often sang in school concerts. When I performed in a concert, Mam sat in the audience. She couldn't hear a single note. Mam also came to watch my school plays. She took her seat but did not hear a single word. She came because that's what other mothers did.

At home, Mam used hands and voice to talk to Roma and me. At our school, Mam never spoke. She did not like to speak in front of strangers. She knew her voice was different.

Did I feel sorry for Mam? No.

Did I feel sorry for myself? No. Deafness was normal in our family.

We were different. That's just the way things were.

When I was a teenager, I owned a bright red plastic radio. I had bought it with babysitting money, and I kept it on a living-room shelf. Every day, I turned it on as soon as I came home from school. When Mam walked into the room, she put her hand on top of my radio. She wanted to see if it was warm, and sometimes she made me turn it off.

"The radio uses too much electricity," she told me.

The real reason, I was sure, was that Mam didn't know what I listened to.

As soon as she left the room, I turned on the radio again. I memorized songs. I sat at the piano and tried to play tunes with one hand.

Seeing me at the piano did make Mam happy. She stood beside me and put her hands on top of the piano. The sound from the keys vibrated through the wood while I tried to play. Mam could feel the music through her hands. That is how she *listened* to music.

Before long, I was able to play songs using both hands. I learned to play by teaching myself.

Mam must have thought I played well. She didn't know how many wrong notes I was hitting. When we had visitors, Mam asked me to play for them. I was too shy to do so because I thought I played badly. Years later, I studied music at university. But when we first owned the piano, I had never taken lessons.

One day, three of Mam's close friends came to visit. Her three friends were deaf. While growing up, they had all attended the Belleville school together. Mam loved having her deaf friends visit. They came once a year when Mam took holidays from work. Her friends stayed at our home for two or three nights.

With four deaf people in the house, all language was signed. Hands moved so quickly, I had to pay attention to keep up. Mam laughed more when her friends visited. By then I was old enough to understand that she was probably really lonely.

Mam asked me to play the piano for her deaf friends. I could not say no, so I sat on the piano bench and started banging away. I tried to play songs I had heard on my radio.

Mam's friends stood close to me and put their hands on top of the piano. They could feel the music. And while I was playing, they suddenly began to dance. The women took off their shoes and danced in bare feet. Vibrations from the music could be felt through the floorboards. We had hardwood floors in our house, and the smooth wood made dancing easy. Mam and her friends twirled around the room. I kept playing. I played every song I knew.

I glanced over at Mam and her friends moving in time to the music, their feet gliding over the floor. They were silent dancers.

One of Mam's friends wore a yellow scarf. She took it off and waved it in the air. Someone else took the other end. The two women danced with the scarf fluttering between them. I tried to watch and play the piano at the same time.

The women moved with grace and joy. They danced by themselves and with one another. When I stopped playing, they stopped dancing. They could no longer feel vibrations through the floor.

I had never known that Mam could dance. I suppose if Father had been alive, I'd have seen my parents dancing. But Father had been dead for many years.

After Mam's friends left, I asked her, "Why didn't you tell me you knew how to dance?"

"Because you never asked," she said.

"What else can you do that I don't know about?" I asked.

"I can do many things that might surprise you and Roma," said Mam.

*

"I've never heard that story," Roma said to her sister. "I love to think of Mam dancing with her friends. Why didn't you tell me before?"

"Because you never asked," said Liz.

Chapter Nine

Wish

After Jessie and Eve left to go home, Liz and Roma cleaned up. They put the dishes away and sat at the kitchen table. Liz poured two glasses of wine.

"I don't know about you, but I'm glad I heard everyone's stories," said Liz.

"I liked meeting your friends," Roma told her. "The way they grew up wasn't so different from the way we did."

"We all became good listeners," said Liz.

"We had good practice. We had to be listeners for our parents," Roma said. "Every one of us."

"A normal part of growing up. Normal in our families, anyway," Liz said.

"Good memory training," Roma said. "Acting as Mam's ears and voice for so many years helps me now. Especially the way I recall people's faces and stories in the clinic where I work."

"And we all speak at least two languages," said Liz. "You and I and Jessie and Eve."

"That's true. We're all bilingual — English and ASL," said Roma. "And most of us speak French, too."

"Do you ever wonder if we had a childhood, Roma?"

"Yes. I sometimes wonder if I was born old."

"You were the first-born," said Liz. "Mam relied on you. You had to mature so quickly."

"I also thought we were the only ones who talked behind our mother's back," Roma said. "Somehow, I feel better knowing that Jessie and Eve did the same."

"I turned up the volume on my radio when I was upset," said Liz. "Just like Eve. Having all that noise around me made me feel better. Even though Mam couldn't hear what I was doing."

"We tried to get away with whatever we could, I guess."

"Do you wish we'd had a different childhood?" Liz asked.

"Not at all. I was so proud of Mam. She raised us by herself after Father died. She worked at the shirt factory all those years."

"And look at the work we do now," said Liz. "You interpret for deaf patients at your clinic. I teach music. Jessie is an ASL interpreter. Eve works with deaf children in theatre. The four of us are in the helping professions."

"That's because we care about other people," said Roma.

"There's something else I'm glad to know," said Liz. "The others longed for store-bought clothes the way we did. Such a small thing, but we wanted them so badly."

"We wanted what we couldn't have," said Roma.

"Mam did sew beautifully. You and I had amazing clothes," said Liz. "But we still wanted something store-bought."

"Eve sure made us laugh, didn't she?" said Roma.

"She's an actor, all right," said Liz.

"She knows how to tell a story," said Roma. "The box on the doorstep, those terrible shoes floating down the river."

"Speaking of boxes," said Liz. "There's still one more box of Mam's things to go through. After her funeral, you and I were pretty tired. We had so many things to do. We went through Mam's house, her closets and clothes. We cleaned floors and washed windows, got rid of furniture, gave things to charity. But one last box had been pushed under the basement stairs. I had to bring it home with me when Mam's house was sold. That last cardboard box is in a closet in my front hall."

"I suppose we could look at it now," said Roma. "One box can't hold that much. Surely it won't take long."

"Bring our wine into the living room," said Liz. "We'll open the box in there."

Liz dragged the box from the hall closet to the living room. The two sisters kneeled on the rug. They opened the flaps of the box and looked inside.

They found old sewing material, folded in layers, along with dress patterns Roma and Liz both remembered. And spools of thread, zippers, and old curtains. Slowly and carefully, the sisters set everything on the rug.

At the bottom of the cardboard box, they saw Mam's old sewing basket. Liz lifted it out and raised the cover. She pulled up a tangle of thread, needles, thimbles, and buttons.

"I'll bet some of these things were bought from the thimble man," said Roma. "Mam kept everything. But look. There's an envelope. What's inside? Something lumpy?"

Liz picked up a worn envelope that lay at the bottom of the basket. She took a quick look inside and passed it to Roma. "There's a note in here," she said. "And something else. I think this is meant for you."

Roma recognized their mother's handwriting. She read out loud, to her sister:

This belongs to Roma. I should have given it to her long ago. The day the wishbone pin dropped in the river, I thought it was lost forever. I went back the next day to see if I could find the things I dropped. Everything had floated away except the wishbone pin, which was partly trapped under a rock near shore. I must have stepped on it when I grabbed baby Liz up out of the water. The pin on the back was bent so badly, I hid the wishbone away. I didn't have the heart to give Roma a broken present for her fifth birthday. But I couldn't throw it out, either. I'm leaving it at the bottom of my sewing basket, where I first hid it. Maybe Roma will find her wishbone pin here some day.

Roma reached into the envelope, and there it was. A slightly crooked wishbone with faded sparkles and coloured stones. The pin on the back was badly bent.

Roma looked at Liz and they both grinned. They clicked their wine glasses.

"Mam really was full of surprises," said Liz. "Looks like she gets the last word tonight."

"She's adding her story to the evening," said Roma. "The end of a story. I can hardly believe the pin was hidden away all those years."

"I suppose you get to make your wish now," said Liz.

"So much time has passed. What I once wished for has changed over the years. Why don't you make a wish, too, Liz? We could both wish for something."

Each sister held a side of the tiny wishbone pin.

"What shall we wish for?" said Liz.

"Listen!" said Roma. "Wishes should never be told. Just close your eyes and think of what you want most. Then don't ever tell a soul. And hope for the best."

Acknowledgements

Many people have shared with me their experiences of deafness in families. I thank the following mothers and daughters: Frances Hill, Carrie Oliver, Jean Stratton, Christine Wilson, Emma Roszak, and Monica Gallivan. Thanks also, Christine, for lending me the original Cook's Book, which belonged to your late mother. What a treasure — and a source for several details in my work of fiction.

For the past fifteen years, I have been reading about Deaf Culture, past and present. Of many books, I acknowledge *Deaf Parents — Hearing Children*, by Lawrence T. Bunde, and *Seeing Voices: A Journey into the World of the Deaf*, by Oliver Sacks. I am also thankful to the many people who devote themselves to listening and watching and ensuring that others will be heard.

Finally, I remember my much-loved grandmother, the late Gertrude Freeman Stoliker. Deaf for 87 of her 88 years, she was the mother of eleven hearing children. And like my fictional characters, my grandmother didn't miss much.

Good Reads

Discover Canada's Bestselling Authors with Good Reads Books

Good Reads authors have a special talent—
the ability to tell a great story, using clear language.

Good Reads can be purchased as eBooks, downloadable
direct to your mobile phone, eReader or computer.
Some titles are also available as audio books.

To find out more, please visit
www.GoodReadsBooks.com

The Good Reads project is sponsored by
ABC Life Literacy Canada.

Grass Roots Press

Good Reads Series

Coyote's Song by Gail Anderson-Dargatz

The Stalker by Gail Anderson-Dargatz

The Break-In by Tish Cohen

Tribb's Troubles by Trevor Cole

In From the Cold by Deborah Ellis

New Year's Eve by Marina Endicott

Home Invasion by Joy Fielding

The Day the Rebels Came to Town by Robert Hough

Picture This by Anthony Hyde

Listen! by Frances Itani

Missing by Frances Itani

Shipwreck by Maureen Jennings

The Picture of Nobody by Rabindranath Maharaj

The Hangman by Louise Penny

Easy Money by Gail Vaz-Oxlade

Coyote's Song
by Gail Anderson-Dargatz

Sara used to be a back-up singer in a band. She left her singing career to raise a family. She is content with being a stay-at-home mom. Then, one Saturday, Sara's world changes.

Sara and her family go to an outdoor music festival. There, on stage, Sara sees Jim, the lead singer from her old band. He invites her to sing with him. Being on stage brings back forgotten feelings for Sara—and for Jim. And Sara's husband Rob sure doesn't like what he sees.

Sara also sees something else: a coyote. Learn how Coyote, the trickster spirit, turns Sara's life upside down.

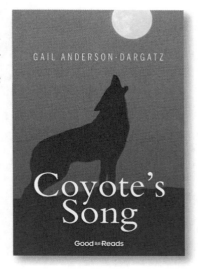

The Break-In

By Tish Cohen

Marcus and Alex have two things in common—they each have a broken heart and a plan.

Marcus wants to win back his girlfriend. He is ready to stage a break-in for her. Eleven-year-old Alex wants to find his father's killer. He has a gun and may be ready to use it.

When Marcus and Alex cross paths, they make a mess. But in a strange way, they also begin to understand each other. *The Break-In* is a funny story about finding brotherhood in dark times.

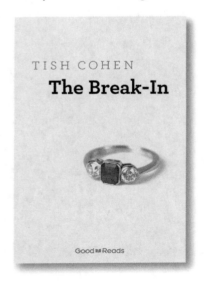

TISH COHEN

The Break-In

Good Reads

Tribb's Troubles

By Trevor Cole

Tribb has always been a thinker, not a doer. But he needs to do something about the mice in his house, and fast.

Linda, his wife, hates those mice. If only Tribb could get rid of the nasty little things. Then Linda might be happy again. Maybe even fall in love with him again.

Tribb has his troubles, all right. Mouse trouble. Marriage trouble. In the end, though, Tribb solves his problems. Or does he?

About the Author

Frances Itani is the author of fifteen books. Among her bestselling novels are *Deafening, Remembering the Bones* and *Requiem*.

Frances taught and practised nursing for eight years. She began to write while studying at university when her children were young. She has worked as a volunteer all her life. Frances lives in Ottawa.

Also by Frances Itani:

Fiction

Truth or Lies

Pack Ice

Man Without Face

Leaning, Leaning Over Water

Deafening

Poached Egg on Toast

Remembering the Bones

Requiem

Missing

Poetry

No Other Lodgings

Rentee Bay

A Season of Mourning

Children's Books

Linger By the Sea

Best Friend Trouble

(forthcoming)

*